P9-DEB-498

AWESOME ATHLETES

LEBRON JAMES

Jill C. Wheeler

ABDO Publishing Company

visit us at
www.abdopublishing.com

Published by ABDO Publishing Company, 4940 Viking Drive, Edina, Minnesota 55435.
Copyright © 2007 by Abdo Consulting Group, Inc. International copyrights reserved in all
countries. No part of this book may be reproduced in any form without written permission from
the publisher. The Checkerboard Library™ is a trademark and logo of ABDO Publishing
Company.

Printed in the United States.

Cover Photo: Corbis
Interior Photos: Al Tielemans/Sports Illustrated p. 14; AP/Wide World pp. 9, 15, 19, 23, 26, 27,
    28-29; Corbis pp. 4, 5, 13, 15, 17, 20, 24, 25; Getty Images p. 10;
    Michael J. LeBrecht II/Sports Illustrated p. 22; Wire Image pp. 7, 14, 21

Series Coordinator: Rochelle Baltzer
Editors: Rochelle Baltzer, Heidi M. Dahmes
Art Direction: Neil Klinepier

Library of Congress Cataloging-in-Publication Data

Wheeler, Jill C., 1964-
  Lebron James / Jill C. Wheeler.
    p. cm. -- (Awesome athletes)
  Includes index.
  ISBN-10 1-59928-306-9
  ISBN-13 978-1-59928-306-7
  1. James, LeBron--Juvenile literature. 2. Basketball players--United States--Biography--
Juvenile literature. 3. African American basketball players--Biography--Juvenile literature.
I. Title. II. Series.

GV884.J36W44 2006
796.323092--dc22   2005035429

Contents

LeBron James

LeBron James is one of the brightest stars in the **National Basketball Association (NBA)**. As a **rookie**, James averaged 20.9 points, 5.5 **rebounds**, and 5.9 **assists** per game. These statistics were as good as those of basketball greats Oscar Robertson and Michael Jordan.

James made a name for himself at a young age. As a freshman in high school, he was compared to some of the best professional

James showed maturity and talent at a young age. An **NBA** scout once described him as "a player who comes around once in every 20 years."

basketball players in history. And as a senior, he was the **NBA**'s number one **draft** pick.

At age 18, James began playing for the Cleveland Cavaliers. The Cavaliers use a five-point scale to rate their players, with five being the best. Coaches judge the players based on their jump height, strength, **agility**, body fat, and speed. One coach says James is a six!

James's impressive shooting range helps him score points from a distance on the court.

James has received praise for other talents on the court, too. He is especially skilled at reading games to know upcoming plays. And, he is always willing to share the ball with his teammates.

In 2005, James became the youngest NBA player to score more than 50 points in one game. James's career is just beginning. He still has time to set more records for the NBA.

Tough Beginnings

LeBron James was born on December 30, 1984, in Akron, Ohio. His mother, Gloria, was young when he was born. So Gloria's mother, Freda, and Gloria's brothers, Terry and Curt, helped her raise LeBron. The James family lived on Hickory Street in one of Akron's poorest neighborhoods.

Although Freda did not have much money, she strongly believed in helping others. When LeBron was eight months old, Freda welcomed a man named Eddie Jackson into their home. Eddie dated Gloria, and he quickly took a liking to young LeBron. To this day, LeBron sometimes refers to Eddie as his father.

For Christmas 1987, LeBron received his first toy basketball set. He loved it. He began dunking the ball right away. However, he would tip over the hoop in the process. So each time, someone would set it up higher. But even with the hoop raised, LeBron was still able to dunk the ball.

The James family wanted LeBron to enjoy that holiday. So, they did not tell him that tragedy had struck early that morning. Freda had died of a heart attack. Only later did LeBron learn that his grandmother was gone.

LeBron loved playing with his toy basketball set. Little did he know that he would be making slam dunks as an NBA superstar one day.

Homeless

Freda had been the family's stabilizing force. Without her, life in the James home unraveled. The James children could not keep up with repairs on the old house. So about two years after Freda's death, the house was declared unfit to live in. Then, it was torn down.

The James family became homeless. The children went their separate ways. Gloria and LeBron headed for Akron's Elizabeth Park public housing **complex**.

Elizabeth Park was located in one of Akron's worst neighborhoods. Violent crimes were not unusual in the area, and police officers were frequent visitors. Young LeBron grew up hearing sirens and gunshots.

Gloria and LeBron moved around to the homes of various friends within Elizabeth Park. Sometimes, they stayed for just a few weeks. Other times, it was a few months. By the time LeBron was five years old, they had moved seven times.

Opposite Page: Gloria and LeBron have always shared a special relationship. Through ups and downs, they have remained close friends.

Fortunately, LeBron made good friends at the **complex**. They helped him stay out of trouble. Sometimes he played sports with them. Yet, LeBron was also comfortable spending time alone.

A Fresh Start

LeBron was nine years old when he started playing organized sports. He joined the local South Rangers peewee football team. During his first year with the team, he scored 18 touchdowns in 6 games! LeBron's coaches were impressed at how quickly he was learning the game.

One of LeBron's coaches was a man named Frankie Walker. Walker became concerned when LeBron did not return to fourth grade after Christmas break. Soon, Walker learned that Gloria was having problems. So, he offered to let LeBron live with him while Gloria got settled. Gloria accepted, and LeBron moved in with the Walkers.

The Walker family brought a sense of order to LeBron's life. LeBron now had a regular bedtime, and he helped with household tasks. He was also expected to complete his homework on time.

At the end of fifth grade, LeBron had a perfect attendance record. He had also earned a B average. Later, LeBron said that living with the Walkers was like a new beginning for him.

By now, LeBron had discovered a new favorite sport. It was basketball. Walker was his first basketball coach. He saw that LeBron stood out from other players. Young LeBron was already able to read the game and think ahead.

Opposite Page: Organized sports provided a sense of stability and focus for LeBron as he grew up. Originally, he wanted to play professional football because of his positive experience with his peewee team.

The Shooting Stars

LeBron began playing amateur basketball in 1995. He was part of the Northeast Ohio Shooting Stars team. He made several good friends on the team. Their names were Dru Joyce, or "Little Dru," Sian Cotton, and Willie McGee. The foursome would play together for many years.

Little Dru's father coached the Shooting Stars. He encouraged the boys to play as a team. The boys pushed each other to become better players. Eventually, they truly clicked together and won national tournaments.

LeBron continued playing with the Stars after entering Riedinger Middle School. By then, Gloria had her own apartment. LeBron lived there with her. They were still in a bad neighborhood. But for LeBron, it was home.

By the end of middle school, **scouts** from various high schools had noticed the talented Shooting Stars. Little Dru, Sian, Willie, and LeBron could have been starters at any high school.

Opposite Page: Throughout his school years, LeBron developed a strong bond with his basketball teammates.

However, the foursome wanted to continue playing together. So when Little Dru decided to attend St. Vincent-St. Mary High School, the others followed. They hoped to win a state basketball championship together.

THE MAKING OF AN AWESOME ATHLETE

LeBron James was tagged a basketball superstar by the time he was a freshman in high school.

1984	1995	1999	2000
Born on December 30 in Akron, Ohio	Begins playing amateur basketball	Enters St. Vincent-St. Mary High School and plays basketball for the Fighting Irish	Leads Fighting Irish to first of three state championships

How Awesome Is He?

James was one of only three NBA rookies to average at least 20 points, 5 rebounds, and 5 assists per game. Since then, he has improved. In the 2005–2006 regular season, James ranked third for scoring.

Player/Ranking	Points Per Game
Kobe Bryant/#1	35.4
Allen Iverson/#2	33.0
LeBron James/#3	**31.4**
Gilbert Arenas/#4	29.3

LEBRON JAMES

TEAM: CLEVELAND CAVALIERS
NUMBER: 23
POSITION: FORWARD
HEIGHT: 6 FEET, 8 INCHES
WEIGHT: 240 POUNDS

2001	2003	2004	2005
Becomes the first sophomore to receive the Ohio Mr. Basketball award	Signs with the Cleveland Cavaliers	Represents the United States in the Summer Olympics	Becomes the youngest NBA player to score more than 50 points in one game

- Attracted such large crowds that ESPN broadcast some of his high school games

- Finished the 2003–2004 season first among rookies in steals, second in scoring, and third in assists

- At age 19, became the youngest NBA Rookie of the Year in 2004

Highlights

High School Sensation

St. Vincent-St. Mary is a private Catholic high school in Akron. It was known for **academics** more than athletics. However, a new basketball coach named Keith Dambrot had recently arrived to lead the St. Vincent-St. Mary Fighting Irish. Dambrot was a former college basketball coach.

During the 1999–2000 season, Dambrot realized he had a talented group of freshmen. However, the players still needed work.

LeBron was now more than 6 feet (2 m) tall and weighed 170 pounds (77 kg)! He could easily muscle his way to the basket. Yet Dambrot knew this would become more difficult as other kids caught up to LeBron's size. So, Dambrot continued to challenge him during practices.

Like earlier coaches, Dambrot saw that LeBron learned quickly. The freshman soon knew more about basketball **strategies** than most college players! LeBron also had a way of making his teammates perform better. Dambrot thought LeBron was the best player he had ever seen.

Opposite Page: During his time at St. Vincent-St. Mary, LeBron would help lead the Irish to many victories.

Struggling with Status

The St. Vincent-St. Mary Fighting Irish ended their 1999–2000 season with a 27–0 record. Freshman LeBron averaged 18 points per game that season. And, the Irish went on to become state champions!

As a sophomore, LeBron appeared in the basketball magazine *SLAM*. Despite the attention, he still devoted time to his team. The Irish finished the 2000–2001 season at 26–1. They won their second state championship in a row! Also that season, LeBron became the first sophomore to win the Ohio Mr. Basketball award.

Meanwhile, LeBron also played football for the Irish. He proved himself a talented wide receiver. He earned all-state honors as a sophomore. As a junior, he helped the team make the state championship semifinals.

As LeBron's athletic success developed, his celebrity **status** grew. Thousands of people focused on him. Competitors began playing the Irish more **aggressively**. Reporters attended the games. And, LeBron found himself surrounded by people wanting his **autograph**.

Reporters often attended Irish games, especially during LeBron's later years at St. Vincent-St. Mary.

As a junior, LeBron made the cover of *Sports Illustrated* magazine. Inside, he was featured in an article headlined "The Chosen One." The article said what many people were already thinking. LeBron could be the one to reenergize the **NBA**. He might be the next Michael Jordan!

Around this time, an overwhelming amount of people wanted to watch the Irish play basketball. So in 2002, the team moved its games to the University of Akron. There, the Irish drew in almost twice as many fans as the university's men's basketball team!

LeBron makes his mark on the court during a home game at the University of Akron

On February 8, 2003, LeBron and the Fighting Irish played in the PrimeTime Shootout. This high school basketball tournament features some of the best U.S. teams and players.

Conflicts

As LeBron's athletic success became more apparent, it was hard for people to treat him like a regular high school student.

LeBron was in a tough position. He was not yet a professional player. And, amateurs are not allowed to accept money or gifts for playing athletics. But many people were already treating him like an **NBA** superstar.

Twice during his senior year, LeBron came close to losing his amateur **status**. If this happened, he could not play for the Irish.

Concerns first arose when LeBron received a Hummer truck from his mother and Jackson. It was a gift for his eighteenth birthday. However, Gloria was still living in **subsidized** housing and did not have a job.

Many people wondered how Gloria had bought LeBron such an expensive present. Some people suggested that someone else had paid for it. However, an investigation showed that Gloria had taken out a loan for the vehicle.

LeBron was questioned again when he received two jerseys worth more than $800. A local shopkeeper had given them to LeBron. Some people believed the shopkeeper gave LeBron the jerseys because

LeBron's friends walked him onto the court before his final game at St. Vincent-St. Mary.

he was an athlete. So, it was ruled that LeBron could no longer play for the Irish.

However, LeBron returned the jerseys and only missed one game. The 2002–2003 season ended as his best yet. He averaged 31.6 points, 9.6 **rebounds,** and 4.6 **assists** per game. The Fighting Irish won their third state championship in four years! Now LeBron could focus on his professional career.

Hello, Cavaliers

During LeBron's senior year, two Fighting Irish games had been broadcast on national television. Meanwhile, the **NBA** was preparing for its **draft**. **Scouts** were out, and LeBron was looking like the favorite.

LeBron was expected to excel, and he didn't disappoint. In his first professional game, he scored 25 points!

The Cleveland Cavaliers had a poor record. In fact, the team tied for the worst NBA record that season at 17–65. None of their games had been broadcast nationally. The only bright spot for the Cavaliers was the upcoming draft. The team's low record meant it had a good chance at getting the number one draft pick.

Sure enough, on June 26, 2003, the Cleveland Cavaliers got LeBron. After graduating from St. Vincent-St. Mary, LeBron signed a three-year, $10.8 million contract with the Cavaliers. However, that seemed small compared to the seven-year, $90 million **sponsorship** deal he made with Nike!

LeBron was the shot of talent that the Cavaliers needed. His presence increased both ticket sales and interest in the struggling team. Most important, LeBron helped the Cavaliers more than double their wins from the previous year! They ended the 2003–2004 season 35–47.

Also in 2004, LeBron participated in the Summer Olympics in Athens, Greece. He was part of the U.S. men's basketball team. The team won the bronze medal.

LeBron with Cavaliers players Darius Miles *(center)* and Ricky Davis *(right)* in November 2003. Coaches believe that LeBron motivates his teammates to play better.

James Today

James volunteered in a local classroom as part of the NBA's Read to Achieve program.

James has come a long way from the streets of Elizabeth Park. He now lives in an 11-bedroom mansion just outside Akron. And, it is estimated that he will earn more than $200 million before he turns 25.

The basketball superstar maintains close ties with his high school friends. He even calls the St. Vincent-St. Mary librarian every now and then. They became friends when she helped him hide from **autograph** seekers at school.

James enjoys activities other than basketball, too. The rising star helps out in his community. In fall 2003, he assisted with the NikeGO Physical Education program. The program aims to increase children's activity levels.

To achieve this goal, the campaign provides athletic equipment to schools.

In January 2006, James participated in the **NBA**'s Read to Achieve program. He visited a local school to read books with sixth grade students. The program promotes reading outside of the classroom. It also encourages adults to read regularly to children.

Bike riders gathered in Akron for LeBron's King for Kids Bikeathon on June 25, 2005. Money earned from the event was given to the Akron Area YMCA and the Akron Urban League.

In many ways, James is like others his age. He often talks to friends on the phone. He likes to play video games and cards. And, he enjoys listening to music. However, James has more responsibilities than many other young men. He has teammates who depend on him. And, he is a role model for people of all ages.

Glossary

academics - subjects taught in school, such as reading, writing, and arithmetic.

aggressive - displaying strong focus and energy.

agility - the ability to move quickly and easily.

assist - a throw or a pass that allows a teammate to score a goal.

autograph - a person's handwritten name.

complex - a building or a group of buildings with related units.

draft - an event during which sports teams choose amateur players.

National Basketball Association (NBA) - a professional basketball league in the United States and Canada that consists of an Eastern and a Western conference, each with two divisions. There are 29 teams in the NBA.

rebound - the act of gaining control of a missed shot in basketball.

rookie - a first-year player in a professional sport.

scout - someone sent to discover new talent, such as athletes or entertainers.

sponsor - someone who pays for a program or an activity in return for promotion of a particular product or brand.

status - a position or rank in a social or professional standing.

strategy - a careful plan or method.

subsidy - a government's grant to a person or a company to assist in an undertaking thought helpful to the public.

Web Sites

To learn more about LeBron James, visit ABDO Publishing Company on the World Wide Web at **www.abdopublishing.com**. Web sites about James are featured on our Book Links page. These links are routinely monitored and updated to provide the most current information available.

Index